Gentleman Jack's Secret Diary for 1817

Anne Lister's encoded journal

Hues Books ISBN 9781909275300

© Patricia Hughes July 2019

Introduction

This book contains only the coded passages of 1817 from Anne Lister's quarto journals. It does not include standard journal entries, or exercise book journals (1806–20th March 1817) or the quarto journals (January 1818-1840). The original journals are held by Calderdale District Archives, reference SH: 7/ML/E/1-26.

For Anne Lister 1817 was a year of letting go of the past and starting again. The coded entries for this year reveal decisions and events that form the rest of her adult life. It was a year of family fatalities, when medicine was very basic and often ineffectual; when a bad cold meant possible death.

Many years before Anne, and/or her lover Eliza Raine, had invented a clandestine code made from the Greek alphabet, punctuation, zodiac and mathematical symbols. Used to record letters and parcels between Anne and Eliza at school in York, it had been originally meant for clandestine notes in school. Anne used it to list their correspondence to ensure that it was not intercepted by authorities.

When their relationship began both girls were 13 years old and boarding at the Manor school in York. For unstated reasons – probably her looming sexuality – Anne had been relegated to a lonely attic bedroom called the 'slope'. Eliza, a potential heiress who was Indian in appearance, joined her a few months later. Rejected from polite society, and sharing a bed in a cold, isolated room, they became very close.

Both were aware of their potential loss of money and independence on marriage, hence their joint decision to live together when grown up, with Anne providing a landed, well-established family and Eliza providing finance.

However in 1806 a teacher discovered their relationship and asked Anne's aunt Anne to remove her from the school as long as Eliza was a pupil. She was allowed to return after her lover had left. Anne moved back to Shibden Hall in Halifax and began listing their letters and parcels.

Over time their assumptions were challenged. When Eliza left school she moved to Halifax where Anne's (and potentially her own) relatives lived But while Anne finished her schooling she began to see that she could find a better partner, and finance could arrive in different ways.

In fact by 1817, through the unexpected deaths of two brothers, she and her younger sister Marian had become the Lister heirs. Despite Anne's continuing low finances, she suddenly had extensive property and influence. By then Anne was known locally as 'Gentleman Jack'.

After discarding Eliza, Anne set her sights on Mariana Belcombe as her life partner. She was a wealthy pupil at school, the daughter of a highly regarded doctor in York.

Dr Belcombe's private mental homes were managed under Quaker precepts. Inmates (including Eliza from 1814) could play the piano, paint and sing; they were treated with respect.

That was in stark contrast to York asylum, which Samuel Tuke had publicly denounced for filthy, primitive conditions and starving inmates. The doctor in charge, Dr Best, was subsequently hounded from his post for incompetence. Deeply upset and depressed, he left for Italy on an extended holiday with his family. Mary, his wife, was the sister of Isabella Norcliffe, Anne's school friend and fellow lesbian in York. The coded passages for 1817 include news of Dr Best's death while abroad.

Anne had promised to live with Eliza, then changed her mind; but when Anne made the same promise to Mariana, it was she who let Anne down. In 1816 Mariana and her mother covertly arranged for her to marry Charles Lawton, a widower with £6000 who wanted an heir. Anne was called away by subterfuge to allow the marriage to take place.

For a few months Anne accompanied the newly married couple, but when Charles learnt of his wife's continuing physical relationship he banished Anne and did his best to prevent Mariana seeing her again. Stung and bereft, Anne returned to Shibden Hall with her aunt and uncle, and began building a new life.

She would continue her education without self-pity, start at 5 am each day. She would recognize her true personality and dress in black, the colour of male dignity and practicality. She would save her sparse finances to take part in her richer friends' social life. Above all she would live a quiet, dignified life and regain the respect of Aunt Anne and Uncle Lister, who managed the Lister estates.

Anne taught herself to be brutally honest about her own character. It allowed her to see through subterfuge, such as that from her Marian's suitor and Miss Jackson. The death of their mother allowed Marian to inherit her mother's farm, so that Anne would be heir to the Lister estates, setting them free from each other's lives.

Anne's alphabetic code contained little punctuation, so I have inserted enough to clarify sentences. I have not altered spellings or syntax. I have done my best to preserve the original meaning.

Patricia Hughes

1817

Friday 21st March   *I propose from this day to keep an exact journal, to accustom me to set a due value on my time.*

Wednesday 2nd April   Had a letter from my mother at Market Weighton saying they had given up the other house in Weighton that they had taken some time ago and were quite unsettled in their plans. No good news about tenants.

Saturday 5th April   My aunt had a parcel from Mariana this morning from Manchester with 8 yds brown silk at 5s per yard and a note written on Thursday in a great hurry to say they were going from thence to Buxton to stay till Monday, and she would write to me as soon as she got home. From 5 to 6 walked with my uncle on the top of Bairstow seeing where Chs. Howarth and Joe Mills measured about the coals.

Saturday 12 April   Busy unpicking a white satin petticoat for Miss Ibbetson to get dyed.

Monday 14th April My aunt lent me five pounds for sundries and pocket money. I must say she is very good to me.

Tuesday 15th April Did not sleep well last night, and was disturbed about 4 by the cook who awoke me to say a shabby-looking man was stealing the hens. In the afternoon walked to Halifax, bought a horse pistol (priced 16/6) at Adam's & Mitchell's, a pound of very large shot 4d, and two ounces powder 3d.

Thursday 24th April My aunt Lister being gone to Elland to see Mrs Greenwood drank tea with my uncle Joseph. My uncle Joseph had a good deal of talk on family affairs. I asked him to make his will. Said I gave the same advice to my uncle Lister and wished him to fear of my mother ever having anything to do with Shibden; to leave it first to my aunt Anne, then to my uncle Joseph, then to my father, and then intail to me.

My uncle Joseph was very communicative. I asked him what was the will he had already made, and he said after leaving my aunt a life estate in the house and an annuity besides, he had likewise left an annuity of fifty pounds a year to my father and my aunt Anne, and the residue and remainder to my uncle Lister. I said he could not do better. He gave me five pounds. I told him it was acceptable for that I had very little from my father and that my aunt and uncle gave me nearly all I had.

Saturday 26th April Had a letter from Mariana. All going on swimmingly as yet, Lawton all attention, gives her all her strengthening medicines and washes her back with *cold water every morning and in spite of his concerns, going to the sea for two months. All this in hopes of a son and heir.*

Stayed ½ hour at Northgate and brought back with me the tin case containing the official copy of the record of our pedigree as it is entered in the College [of Arms].

Wednesday 30th April   Had a letter from Marian (Market Weighton) directed by my father containing an inclosure of five five-guinea East Riding bank notes. I read my uncle and aunt the letter and showed them four of the notes but said nothing of the fifth. This is a sort of dissimulation which my heart does not approve and I already repent having practiced it, but I is not pleasant not to have a sixpence but what they know of, as I may occasionally want a pound or two extraordinary, witness my lending Anne Belcombe a pound or two when she was here last autumn.

My mother went to York on Monday by the 9 o'clock morning coach meaning to be back in the evening, but my father thought she would stay all day particularly as she talked of going to see Mr. Dales. This sort of thing annoys me, but I am determined not to be much in York again for one while.

Friday 2nd May   Immediately after breakfast walked to Halifax went to Arkwith the taylor in Gibbet-Lane and paid him out of the money my father sent me (£12), to discharge a bill of his against my father dated 15th Sept. 1815, amounting to £12-0-4d.

Walked on to Stoney Royde and sat an hour with Mrs. Rawson. It was the common topic of conversation that

Mariana was parted from Charles Lawson and returned to her father and mother, that she and Charles were the most miserable couple in the world and that in fact he had little or nothing, that he had killed his first wife, had not the best character, etc. etc. in short, the old over again. I pretended to smile at the strange incongruity of reports and made the matter look as well as I could, but surely in spite of anything I could say people would think there would not be all these reports afloat without some reason or other.

Saturday 3rd May   I am to begin my letter to Mariana as usual but not send it till the latter end of next week or the Monday of the following week instead of next Monday."Charles has taken it into his head lately to go for the letters and sometimes we do not get them till 12 or 1. Till this whim ceases perhaps a little irregularity may be as well."

Monday 5th May   After dinner fired off the pistol that had been heavily charged above three weeks out of my room window. The report was tremendous! It bounded out of my hand, forced itself through the window and broke the lead and 2 panes of glass. My hand felt stunned for some time.

Wednesday 7th May   At ¼ before six went to drink tea at the Greenwoods at Cross Hills. Miss Caroline Greenwood enlarged on the value she set on my notes and rallied me on the shortness of her last. She would like to have long ones from me and longed to see some of my letters, regretted the "invisible enchantment" that kept me so closely at Shibden, often longed to put on her things and join me when she saw me go past and threatened to do so sometime or other. In fact she makes a dead set – to all which I return as encouragement but am very civil.

Friday 9th May My uncle went to meet Hinchcliffe, Walsh & Sutcliffe and received from them in payment for coals £90 annual rent and for a road £10.

Monday 12th May Spent the greatest part of the time looking over plans of the estate and hearing my uncle read over the rates of assessment of the township of Southowram.

Tuesday 13th May I would rather be a philosopher than a polyglot and mean to turn my attention eventually and principally to natural philosophy. For the present I mean to devote my mornings before breakfast to Greek and afterwards till dinner to divide the time equally between Euclid and arithmetic then commence my long-neglected algebra. I must read a page or two of French now and then. The afternoons and evenings are set apart for general reading, for walking ½ an hour or ¾ practice on the flute.

Wednesday 14th May Mr. Wiglesworth came to tea to ask my uncle to go and vote for Scott. Hawksworth was 50 ahead last night and as his friends are not over nice about votes he seems to every chance of getting in. Stocks sent Thomas and William Greenwood and their votes were taken, though their £100 per annum freehold must be in the skies if anywhere. Hawksworth has a strong party in Craven, the ladies there have been busy canvassing for him for some time.

Saturday 17th May   The town was very busy, quite a crowd about Mr. Edward's the booksellers'. He has given the mob three 36 gallon barrels of strong ale, was met by a band of 12 or 14 musicians last night at 10 o'clock as he came from Wakefield, has had this band parading all over the town both today and yesterday, and his wife pastes on all the little boys' hats orange papers with the inscription 'Hawksworth for ever'.

Monday 19th May   Had a letter from Mariana. Charles continues terribly jealous of me. Mariana thinks we had better be cautious lest he should forbid her writing to me and therefore desired to hear from me every other Tuesday. I see there will be little comfort for Mariana and me as long as he lives and God knows how long that will be.

Thursday 22nd May   I shall write to Mariana this morning and send it on Saturday or Sunday. God help those who are tied to such people! I wish the day was over. Nothing but keeping my mind so intent upon study can divert the melancholy reflections which would constantly prey upon me. Alas! They are even now a source of bitterness and disquiet that words can ill describe. Wrote 2 ½ pages to Mariana chiefly in our secret alphabet which I have lately in my letters to her used a great deal.

Saturday 24th May   Charles has been in one of his humours again and they had a row. In consequence of the agitation Mariana so ill she could hardly hold her head up all Sunday and Monday. Filled my letter chiefly in *character cipher which took me from 1 till 2 and till near 5 in the afternoon.*

Wednesday 28th May   Had a note from Mrs Edwards, Pye Nest, to ask me to a supper party and to stay all night on the 4th of next month. Wrote an answer to be ready for the post in the afternoon declining all parties but saying I hoped to spend a long day with her in a friendly way as soon as my aunt returned from Harrogate.

Sat up talking to my uncle till 11 o'clock about getting married, mentioning the wishes of Mr and Mrs and Miss Marsh for me to have Sir George Stainton. My uncle exclaimed all unaware "Well then there will be no occasion for the pedigree I think." Except this he hardly said a word. It is his general custom when you tell him anything never to speak for fear of committing himself as he calls it. I took care however to say that I never intended to marry at all. I cannot make out whether he suspects my situation towards Mariana. In the course of conversation I said "Well I think I could get on with Perce as well as anybody" but he did not apparently notice it. What will be my fate God knows. I begin to despair that Mariana and I will ever get together, besides I sometimes think she will be worn out in the don's service and perhaps I may do better. Heaven only knows how it will end.

Saturday 31st May   A card from Mr & Mrs Greenwood asking my uncle & me to dinner on Wednesday. Wrote a note to decline the invitation.

Sunday 1st June   I have almost made up my mind always to wear black.

Thursday 5th June   Finding I could not attend to arithmetic, my mind being so entirely engrossed with Mariana, I began my epistle to her. I somehow or other in spite of her assurances of love and hope begin to despair that we shall ever get together. We have no chance of seeing much of each other so long as the don lives and may probably not meet for some years to come. What effect such a length of separation may have God knows, the thought made me so low that I cried and wrote alternately the whole morning. I do not doubt Mariana's affection but tis sad to live upon love so hard as this and many are the hours when I am wretched.

Monday 9th June   Read to end Olinth. 3. Demosthenes' and Leland's translation. This is the 4th Greek work I have read through and I certainly feel considerably improved but I am dissatisfied with myself for not having lately got up in a morning as early as I ought. It grieves me that I am ever in bed after 5.

Thursday 12th June   Had a letter from my mother (Market Weighton) giving a dismal account of things at Skelfler and Low Farm. Not a sixpence of rent to be got from the tenant at either place. It must be confessed that my mother writes sensibly enough – she is oftener right in some things than my father chooses to allow. Spent the rest of the afternoon and evening talking over the contents of my mother's letter and proposing plans for improvement, mentioned too settling the estate upon Marian and myself or putting it out to nurse. My uncle as usual on these occasions said little or nothing but at heart he seemed to think what I said reasonable.

Saturday 14th June My uncle Joseph taken ill last night (his old complaint inward bleeding), he has bled a great deal.

Sunday 15th June My uncle Joseph rather better than he was yesterday. My uncle Lister called before and after afternoon church and he and I walked home to tea talking about my uncle Joseph's and my father's concerns.

Monday 16th June Had a long letter from Mariana dated Conway (Wales) Mon 9th June. Had a long letter also from Isabella Norcliffe (Naples) dated 25th May; they were to leave Naples the following day for Rome, thence to proceed to Florence, Nice, Berne & Bruxelles on their way home. She gives a tolerable account of herself and writes affectionately as ever. Ah my dear Isabella you have indeed loved me truly, and after all it may be fate that you and I shall get together at last, God knows what is best. I love Mariana but endless obstacles seem to rise up against this connection. I wonder if Isabella is improved.

Tuesday 17th June My uncle Joseph very considerably better and in good spirits, my uncle Joseph, my aunt Lister and I had a good deal of conversation about Weighton concerns. I asked my uncle's advice about the propriety of suggesting to my father the advantage of making some settlement and of leaving Weighton etc. and was much pleased to find him entirely of my opinion. He mentioned some retired part of Scotland or Wales as a residence. All this we talked over at home when I got back and my sentiments strengthened by the concurrence and approbation of my uncle Joseph.

Sunday 22nd June   After breakfast finished my letter to Mariana, the first letter in which I have written nothing in our new alphabet since we invented it, perhaps I may not make much use of it in future.

Saturday 28th June   In the evening between 6 and 7 my father arrived having come on horseback from Market Weighton, brought no letters, walked down to Northgate, found my uncle Joseph not quite so well and in low spirits.

Monday 30th June   Sent my letter to my mother in answer to her last letter received Thurs 12 June and had a letter from Mariana giving a long account t of the excursion she and her sister Louisa made into North Wales the week before last. They very much admired Lady Eleanor Butler's and Miss Ponsonby's cottage near Llangollen. Mariana wished we had such a one.

*   I now begin to think seriously that she and I will never get together. Strange to say I feel as if I was weening myself from wishing it. I begin to fancy I shall not like another man's leavings and that by the time Charles is out of the way I may have suited myself as well all things considered. I have no fault to find with Mariana as to her conduct but her letters have ceased to be those best calculated to keep alive my affections and the present impossibility of our seeing each other   may have made a wide difference in both before we meet again. I love her yet still I never felt till now that I could love without her. God knows how the thing will end. I feel a sad want of someone and I am sure I will be anxious to fix as soon as I have a fortune and establishment of my own. Mariana feels secure of me but she may change her mind. I cannot forget the*

trick she once played. I am convinced that nothing but this want of confidence could ever have changed me to what I am but I will endeavour not to think of it and will let the thing take its chance.

Saturday 5th July   Did 3 of the arithmetic questions over again that I did so stupidly on Tuesday. Understood them and did them properly today. Had a letter from Mariana. Charles was ill last Saturday and Sunday and Mariana went with him at a moment's warning on Monday to Manchester to see Dr Hull of that place who put him on a meagre diet. If Charles was to be taken off soon, if she & I were thus brought together and I found her affectionate as ever I am sure all my former love and confidence would soon return.

Sunday 6th July   Wrote a few lines to my mother to ask if she will have the silk she sent by my father dyed black as it will not take a brown.

Monday 7th July   After breakfast walked to Stoney Royde, found Ellen looking fat and well and good-humoured and glad to see me as ever. Her little girl Marian grown one of the prettiest children I ever saw and the boy William Henry four months old, a fine child enough. Stayed till near 8 in the evening.
Ellen walked with me up the old bank as far as the top of it. We had a great deal of confidential conversation as we walked along. Among other things I asked her what their housekeeping cost them; she said the last two years £12,000 but they did not mean it to be so much in future as they had bought a good deal of furniture and stacked their

cellars. She thought the articles of housekeeping did not exceed £600 but that Mr Empson's [her husband's] horses with their attendant expenses cost £100 a year apiece. However she said even as times were now they had £1400 a year to spend, Mr Empson had seven and she had seven allowing in her own case for the rise in funds for that their father had left his children £16000 apiece, a large sum she observed to have made from nothing, and that if he had lived a year longer it would have made a difference in the value of his funded property to the amount of fifty thousand pounds. Mt Empson had considerable expectations from the death of his aunt Mrs Hotham. Ellen said how well Christopher Saltmarshe and her sister Emma were off; they could afford to spend near £1500.

There is a great deal of native candour and charming simplicity about Ellen. I could not help being foolish enough to let my conversation manifest this. I told her in what consisted my oddity, reminded her she used to say she liked me better for it and asked her if she wished me to change. She answered she still liked me fir it and would not have me change at all. I told her that I could not say that her marriage had at first given me pleasure; I said my regard for her was greater perhaps than she once suspected and would never change. She made the same profession. She certainly did not seem to dislike any part of my conversation, nor did she in the least discourage it.

I promised to spend a little while with her in the East Riding but plainly hinted that I did not much like the neighbourhood on my mother and father's account. She said she never hears of them. I answered no, I daresay not. Ellen said [her brother] Tom and her uncle William were as much as ever gulled by Mr Colbeck; Mr William

Rawson wants both Ellen and Emma to lend him five hundred pounds. Ellen cannot because her trustees (her brothers Christopher Stanfield and William Henry) will not consent.
I had altogether a pleasant day and only regret being so foolish as to hint at those sentiments which I myself wonder at considering my situation towards Mariana and Isabella but I am determined this shall be the last time I ever hint at anything of this sort to Ellen, after all I don't know that I care much about her. What a strange being I am.

Thursday 10th July   My father came into my room just after I got upstairs and stayed to write a letter to his tenant about paying the rent.

Saturday 12th July   This idleness makes me unhappy and yet my mind is so unhinged I do not feel as if I could do much this morning. I began thinking how little confidence I had in Mariana, I was very low. I felt that my happiness depended on having some female companion whom I could love and depend on and my thoughts naturally turned to Isabella. I got out her picture and looked at it for ten minutes with considerable emotion. I almost wished I could so manage her temper as to be happy with her.
Mrs and Miss Caroline Greenwood called on my aunt but I did not make my appearance. My uncle Joseph rode up and sat above an hour. He seemed tolerable.
          My roaring bout in the morning did me good; I feel my spirits rather better though I am well convinced my only chance of comfort is in rigorous, unrelaxed occupation

of mind. I must rouse myself by every argument of emulation and study as hard as I can.

Sunday 13th July   We all went to church. Rain came on during service and we were obliged to borrow umbrellas. My aunt dined at Northgate and found my uncle much the same as yesterday. In the afternoon and evening besides reading the service as we always do, read aloud the first 2 sermons of 'Sermons' by the Reverend R. Polwhele.

Wednesday 16th July   My uncle and aunt drank tea at the Prescott's, my father and I stayed at home, indeed I was not asked, I suppose from its being known that I decline parties, at all events they might have given me the option of refusing.
My uncle and aunt got home a little after 10. Neither Mr nor Miss Prescott made any enquiries after me, that probably their not inviting me was an intentional omission and rudeness, I know not what for.

Friday 18th July   This idleness is terrible, I know not when I shall get into the way of waking every morning at 5.

Saturday 19th July   A letter from Mariana written in rather low spirits and expressing a sorrow for the ill humour of her last which hurts me ten times more than the ill humour itself. She says speaking of the enormous price she has paid for the conveniences of this world "Do not you forsake me and I shall still stand erect." This sentence does indeed go to my heart.

Sunday 20th July   Walked to Lightcliffe, got there by 10 o'clock, went to both morning and afternoon church and spent a very pleasant day with Mr and Mrs Priestley. I really think she is almost the only gentlewoman in this town; from her manner and conversation I should judge she likes me. I am determined to pay her every attention just to see how far I can prejudice her in my favour. Surely I have not quite lost the art of praising the ladies?

Monday 21st July   My uncle Joseph was very poorly yesterday and has not been better today.

Friday 25th July   In the morning had a letter from Marian (Market Weighton) giving a long history of her going fishing with a Miss Jackson to whom she seems to have taken a fancy and two of her brothers, daughter and sons of a Major Jackson of the Marines, a gentlemanly man I understand, who for economy's sake has taken lodgings at Market Weighton.

    Just before getting into bed read thirty-one pages of (I got it out of the library) "French pox with all its kinds, causes, signs and prognosticks; also the running of the veins, chanker, bubogleets and their cures ... all comprised in this fifth edition of Little Venus Unmasked ... by G. Harvey M. D."

Monday 28th July   My uncle Joseph likely to continue much the same for some time i.e. very dropsical as he always is after his attacks of inward bleeding and teased with a very bad anasarchous cough.

Thursday 31st July   All the afternoon and evening during supper writing out the index to my little note book which owing to the multiplicity of little articles has been

very tedious – even now I have only arranged the rough draft alphabetically. Torrents of rain during the night and also this day with a good deal of thunder about noon.
Saturday 2nd August   A letter from Mariana as usual, not quite what I think it might and should have been, in fact I am generally disappointed with her letters.

Called for five minutes at Horley Green to tell Miss Ralph that her friend Miss Ann Caldwell of Linley Wood was married on Wednesday last to a Mr Marsh, a banker in London, a very private wedding so that none of the neighbours knew anything about it as Mariana says in her letter.

Sunday 3rd August   None of us went to church in consequence of the weather. My uncle drank tea at Northgate and found my uncle Joseph very poorly, low and more swelled than ever. In the afternoon wrote to Mariana. On second thoughts I thought it better not to send what I wrote yesterday and have therefore written a letter touching very slightly but kindly on those parts of Mariana's letter which did not quite please me; there was a vein of joking sarcasm which I have intirely avoided today. I am determined I will never write anything that can give any kind of uneasiness or that I need wish recalled.

Friday 8th August   Had a letter from Miss Marsh (Micklegate, York) who has just had a letter from Turin giving very bad accounts of Dr. Best [Isabella's brother-in-law].

Saturday 9th August   Spent the evening in conversation; talked seriously of going to Mr Knight [vicar and former *tutor] again and no sort of objection being made, but rather the contrary, I think I shall do it as soon as my uncle Joseph is sufficiently better.*

Sunday 10th August   Wrote a few lines to my mother to say my father would prolong his stay a little on my uncle Joseph's account. Uncle Joseph was in bed from the fatigue of being harassed in the night by medicine; by way of diuretic he is taking squills and elaterium to which is added some aperient.

Tuesday 12th August   Found Mr Knight at home; on mentioning my wish to become his pupil again he said he could not take me till after Michaelmas but would then let me have an hour from 3 to 4 every other day according to my desire. Mr Knight was gone to the Bell's school, Dr Bell having unexpectedly come over to inspect it and found very great faults, called both the master and the governess blockheads, so that the man and he came to very high words. I have seen him several times at York, saw him frighten a poor master and his Sunday scholars half out of their wits. I heard some authentic anecdotes of him as to temper and running round the garden to kiss and pay court to Miss Sarah Telford, a young girl not half his age. Dr. Bell afterwards married a lady more of his own age said to have has £12000 but they were separated soon after the match and have continued so ever since.

Monday 18th August   My father gave me seven pounds which led me to reckon up my money and I found that I had altogether twenty-eight pounds, seven shillings and five pence, such a sum I have not had together of years, not since I went to Bath in 1813, and I take good care to let nobody know I have so much. Looked into Emerson's mechanics for ¼ hour as I wish to prepare myself a little for Dalton's lectures, which are to begin on Thursday and which I mean to attend.

Tuesday 19th August   John Oates of the Stump came; his errand was a pair of spectacles for my aunt. I was surprised to find him such a good workman and optician – entirely self-taught – he learnt Latin and Greek at Hipperholme school and afterwards became a good arithmetician and algebraist as well as pretty well versed in Euclid. What a pity such a man should have been put apprentice to a card-maker, then have turned tanner and should now be a banksman at a coal-pit! The pit to be sure is his own at least; he and John Green of Mytholm have jointly taken it of my uncle Lister. It seems his name is not unknown as Richard Dalton the lecturer (for which I bought a ticket priced 14s this afternoon) called on him the other day and made him the offer of a ticket gratis and begged him to attend his lectures. He has made several telescopes, large electrifying machines etc. all excellent. He now lives in a neat house that he built some years ago at the Stump and is comfortable in his circumstances owing to the frugality of his parents who saved their money at the Mytholm public house and by his own prudence in keeping what he had.

Wednesday 20th Aug.   Just after breakfast received a box containing the little alabaster cupid on a bed of roses which Isabel mentioned having sent to me in her letter. Poor Isabel! She never forgets me. I can confide in her affection *and this is more than I can say of Mariana, I cannot forget Mariana's conduct in the autumn of 1814.*

The lecture pretty well attended, there might be 50 including 8 or 20 of Miss Watkinson's young ladies. On the whole I was quite as well satisfied as I expected.

Saturday 23rd August A letter from Mariana to say she had not written last week in consequence of going to Buxton, and one from Isabella dated Tende at the foot of the Alps saying Dr Best expired there about two o'clock in the morning of 30th of July last. "Poor Charles [Best]" says Isabel "had a particular aversion to be buried in the English burying-ground at Nice and had taken a great fancy to a ruined monastery within a mile or two of this place, but on sending to ask permission it was refused, in consequence of which poor Mary [his widow] set off to carry him to Nice and from thence to Leghorn to the English burying-ground there. This morning brought a letter from Charlotte [Isabel's sister] saying they were subject to a quarantine of 40 days. Fortunately Mary remembers him once slightly to have expressed a wish to be buried near the Light-House at Nice; she is therefore determined to deposit his remains there."

Wednesday 27th Aug. Went to the lecture at seven. Having all the four preceding nights admired Miss Brown, daughter of Mr Copley Brown of West Field, sat just before her, handed her several things to look at and contrived to get into conversation with her. I stayed a good while afterwards to look at the apparatus or rather at Miss Brown.

Put my letter to Isabella into the post. Vide a copy of a few of the concluding lines: "I can't bear that in this season of affliction your nearest and dearest friend should seem unconnected in distress. Do tell me you have assured Mary that if sympathy for her sorrows and ardent prayers for her resignation and the welfare of her children can make deserved the name of friend she has not a more sincere one than myself."

Thursday 28th August Did nothing but dream of Miss Brown and though I awoke at six yet had not resolution to get up but lay dozing and thinking of the fair charmer. She is certainly very pretty, she seemed evidently not displeased with my attention and I felt all possible inclination to be as foolish as I ever was in former days, in fact I shall be much better out of her way than in it. My father left us soon after breakfast. Emma Saltmarshe and her bride's maid Miss Margaret Markland called in the morning. Miss M is a good-tempered girl, she and I got very good friends, so much so that I took her up in my arms and jumped her over a puddle-hole in the road.

Friday 29th August   Sat directly behind Miss Brown and talked to her ten minutes after the lecture was over. She evidently seems flattered by my notice and well she may for I do not notice anyone else much. I must say my attention to Miss Brown has been pointed these last two nights, I wonder if anyone has observed it?

Saturday 30th August   A letter from Mariana. We are as it were cut off from each other. The thought of this and one thing or another made me so low I cried for an hour.

Monday 1st September Got to the lecture by seven. As usual talked to Miss Brown, asked her if she would be at the next – No! she was going to Harrogate on Wednesday. (I said) "A ball is a great attraction, and after all we have just been hearing like things have strong affinities, and one's attractions therefore must strongly attract another." I could not discover from her countenance whether she took the compliment or not, she made no reply.

Tuesday 2nd September Spent the whole morning in vamping up a pair of old black chamois shoes. As soon as I was dressed went to drink tea with the Miss Walkers of Cliff Hill – went in black silk, the first time to an evening visit I have entered upon my plan of always wearing black.
Sunday 7th September In my letter to Mariana enclosed the two-pound bank of England notes in payment of a bill of £3-19-6 for 18 yards bombasin at 2/2d for my aunt and 7 yards of black silk at 6/9d for myself got in Manchester.

Monday 8th Sept. Had a letter from Miss Marsh to say she had paid for my hat at Mrs Cooke's in Coney Street 15s and 2s the deal-box. After tea walked to Horley Green to call upon the Ralphs'. Mr James Stansfeld (about to marry Emma) walked home with me.

Wednesday 10th Sept. Offered to pay my aunt the two-pound bank of England note she lent me on Sunday to send to Mariana for the black silk. She would not take it but gave me back the money again that I am two pounds richer than I expected to be. Stayed talking to my aunt about what things I should want: gowns. Petticoats spending money etc.

Thursday 11th Sept.   Wrote to Miss Marsh (York) to thank her for paying Mrs Cooke for me and to ask her to pay my friendly society subscription as soon as it becomes due. Enclosed a one-pound bank of England note (no. 40698 Jan 31st 1815 S. Draper) and 8 shillings and 2 sixpences neatly sewed up in paper every one separately and in two rows to fit the shape of the letter.

Saturday 13th Sept.   (While staying at Haugh End for the weekend with Mrs William Priestley a.k.a. Mary) A thousand reflections and recollections crowded on me last night. The last time I slept in this room was with Mariana (in 1815 the summer). I fondly thought my love and happiness would last forever, alas! How changed. She has married a blackguard for the sake of his money, we are debarred all intercourse.

Sunday 14th Sept.   In conversation about economy and keeping house Mary told me last year they spent above seven hundred pounds though it was not an expensive year and it did not appear that they could live as they do for less.

Monday 15th Sept.   Downstairs and breakfast and all packed by ½ past 9. Felt a good deal tired with my ride, rode double behind William on Diamond.

Friday 19th Sept.   My uncle Joseph was tapped by Mr Sunderland, there were taken from him rather upwards of 7 quarts of water; he was not at all sick, bore the operation very well. My aunt Lister overcome with anxiety and agitation of spirits fainted the moment she was told it was well over.

Saturday 20th Sept.   My uncle as well as could be expected after the operation of tapping but seems likely to fill again in the course of a few weeks.

Sunday 21st Sept.   The orifice which appeared quite closed yesterday burst open again, and in consequence of the uncomfortableness occasioned by the oozing out of the water my uncle Joseph went to bed again in a great passion and very irritable at being troubled again when he expected it was all done with.
Wrote to Mariana, concluded "God bless you Mariana, I am very sick but my heart is yours and well as ever." This is the first time in my life I ever felt any remorse in saying anything affectionate to Mariana, I do not feel to have written truth, I do not think of her much, I rather incline to Isabella, I hope to form some new and more desirable connection. My connection with Mariana is certainly bad as to family. Time alone can tell.

Thursday 25th Sept.   Directly after dinner walked to the library then went to Northgate and spent the afternoon and drank tea there; my uncle Joseph sitting up in one of the front rooms upstairs looking better than I expected, and the running of water from the orifice almost abated.
    During tea, speaking of the attention she had always paid my uncle etc. etc., told me to my no small astonishment that she had never had any connection with him since his first attack of hemorrhage (that is for the last nineteen years); she said he had never shewn the least inclination for it and had never had any erection (meaning of the penis); that she was assured he had had no connection with any woman during these nineteen years

and that in point of virility he was not worth much. The circumstance is conclusive enough, especially as it has not been at all my aunt's fault!

Saturday 4th October   My uncle (Lister) seems now to have made up his mind about entailing the estate, he mentioned his determination at breakfast and said he would do it but that it might be as well to wait awhile to see how my uncle Joseph went on.

Sunday 5th October   My uncle Joseph very poorly today, told my aunt Anne he felt he could not live longer and mentioned several things respecting his decease – what bills he owed etc. My uncle Lister called on his way from afternoon church; my uncle Joseph gave him his will to take home.

Thursday 9th October   Fanny (the housemaid at Northgate) yesterday asked Mr Daniel Mitchell one of (the surgeon's) Mr Sunderland's apprentices what they thought of her master. He said he might live 3 months or 3 weeks or less but that "his inside was quite gone."

Tuesday 14th October   In the morning sorted out all Isabella's letters to me from 1810 to the autumn of 1816.

Wednesday 15th Oct.   My aunt Anne dined at Northgate today; my uncle Lister went down in the morning to witness and see my uncle Joseph sign some powers of attorney in readiness to sell out his funded stock. Got in 15 hattocks of wheat this morning, the last of our this year's harvest.

Thursday 16th Oct. No time for the flute. This general rummage among my letters and papers takes a great deal of time but tis high time to begin if I mean to get it done in my life time.

Saturday 18th Oct. From a little before tea till near 11 at night looking over poor Eliza Raine's letters. My heart bled at the remembrance of the past, poor girl! She did indeed love me truly.

Sunday 19th Oct. Wrote a letter to Mariana asking her to make a parcel of all the letters she has had of mine up to the present time and send them from Manchester the next time they go. I added "a miniature would do much to make me happy".

Tuesday 21st Oct. Looking over the correspondence between Mariana and me at the close of 1814 and beginning of 1815. She certainly behaved very ill and very inconsistently. It seems a strange mixture of selfishness and weakness. I trust to grow wiser in the future.
Paid Mrs Farrer (the dressmaker) a bill of my mother's 7/7 ½ d dated 23rd April 1815.

Wednesday 22nd Oct. Looking over the correspondence between Mariana and me in the beginning of 1815: whatever might be her regard for me it is very plain it bore but a very subservient portion to her regard for the good things of this world. I was in love or surely I could not have been so blinded and acted with such doting folly. Oh that I then could have given her up without a struggle.

Thursday 23rd Oct. My aunt gave me five pound notes and my uncle five pounds in silver. Looking over my money and arranging these matters till considerably after 12. My aunt only knows of my having eleven pounds nine shillings and sixpence but I have besides a hoard of two five-guinea East Riding notes, Bowers bank three pound notes, Rawson's two gilt guineas, fifteen shillings and sixpence in silver and five quite new shillings and eight quite new sixpences, making altogether sixteen pounds sixteen shillings and sixpence.

Sunday 26th Oct. My uncle Joseph was at up with last night for the first time, Fanny till 1¼ and Thomas the rest of the night, and had a bad night. Dr Paley and Mr Sunderland found him very poorly. Had a letter from Marian to say Mrs Inman had caught a bad cold after her confinement which had flown to her right breast, that it had suppurated and though this relieved her, Dr Inman thought her in imminent danger and that I might expect every post to hear of her death.

Monday 3rd November Added the following to my letter to Mariana: "I have been thinking my love as you are so hurried, I will be content to hear from you only every other Saturday. What think you of this plan Mary? It will leave you rather more at liberty." Called to enquire after Mr Knight, resumed the subject of my studies, of how much I had forgotten and how little he was to expect, and it was agreed that I should recommence my attendance on him tomorrow at 3 o'clock. I am to go Tuesdays Thursdays and Saturdays.

Tuesday 4th November I construed Greek Mr Knight said pretty well – a proof he added of what he expected, that I had lost less Greek than Latin. He confessed however he had not given me the easiest Latin to read. The real fact is Mr Knight does not well remember what progress I had formerly made, I am just now a better Grecian than I ever was in my life. As for Latin whatever I may have lost is certainly not in construing, it is perhaps in writing it. Algebra is to come on Thursday; I have lately done the first six books of Euclid twice over and 30 propositions of the Data.

Thursday 6th November   Mr Edwards had just been at the sale at Hodsack Priory near Blythe in Nottinghamshire of the furniture, books etc. belonging to the late Mr Mellish who died about six months ago. Everything was sold, even pictures painted by himself and Mrs Mellish's harp and piano. She (the widow) will not have a sixpence left and the creditors will not get a shilling in the pound as the estate goes to his sister Mrs Chambers, a widow and her son. She is now in Italy and Mrs Mellish is gone to her. Hodsack Priory and the estate that remains between 2 and 3,000 acres was secretly entailed on Mrs Chambers by Mr Mellish himself immediately on the sale of the Blythe estate (which sold for £96,000) to Mr Walker, this was of course a great blank to his creditors.

Went to Mr Knight's at 3. The first sum he set me was in algebraic addition; I made light of this so he set me some sums in algebraic long division and fractions and gave me a couple of algebraic theorems to work, very easy, and here my examination ended. He said nothing to this effect but I was obviously much better than he expected.

Friday 7th November   William brought an account of my uncle Joseph at ½ past 9 saying he had thrown up blood last night every hour as regularly as the clock struck and was very ill indeed this morning. Letter from Marian to say Mrs Inman continued just the same, that Dr Belcombe when "asked if he thought she is ever to be restored, replied he could not tell". Marian says the child (the little boy) died this morning. Marian mentions also my mother being ill having got a very bad cold, had the cramp in her stomach and a bad pain in her right side for which she was just going to put on a blister.

Saturday 8th November   Thomas came up about 9 to say my uncle Joseph died a few minutes past one this morning. My aunt Anne went to Northgate immediately, my uncle and I followed at 11. My uncle went into the room to them directly but was so overcome he was obliged to hurry out again. Wrote a few lines to my father by this morning's post to announce the melancholy event and say if he could leave my mother there was no time to be lost. At 3 o'clock Milne the undertaker and Casson the joiner and the sexton came. My aunt Lister saw Mr Milne and was more composed than I had any idea she could be. Mrs Stead the mantua-maker came; chose mourning. The servants had each 8 yards wide twilled stuff at 2/4d and 3 ½ yards of the same for a petticoat. Fanny brought in the melancholy intelligence of the Princess Charlotte of Wales having died a few hours after being brought to bed of a still-born male child on Thursday.

Sunday 9th November Before breakfast wrote a couple of pages to Miss Marsh to tell her of my uncle Joseph's death.

Wrote my aunt the copies of two letters; gave my uncle a copy of what he should send to the London papers. Wrote also 2 ½ pages to Mariana and was just going to seal it when William brought me a letter from her saying she had been distracted with the toothache – durst not let Woolfenden draw the teeth, they were so broken; Charles had made her an offer of going to York to have McLean and asked my advice whether to go or not. To this I hastily replied "Self-preservation is the law of nature, I see no objection to your going to York." Just before going to bed drank Isabella's health and happiness, it being her 32nd birthday.

Monday 11th Nov.   Wrote a few lines to Marian to say my father arrived safe. Had mourning sent over from Farrer's and bought our own two women servants 17 ¼ yards (the cook being so big takes 9 ¼ yards). I made a point of being civil to Miss Tennant (who brought hats) as being the daughter of Dr Belcombe's sister, inquired after her mother who is a sort of teacher to the Miss Ibbetson, sister of the two Miss Ibbetsons the milliners who opened a boarding and day school in this town about two years ago. Wednesday 12th Nov. My father had a letter from Marian, "My mother in great danger yesterday, she is still however very ill." I told my father how much I was shocked and surprised at this account as Marian's letter of Saturday to my aunt had not at all led me to believe my mother in any danger. I told my father that in such a case he ought not to have been so afraid of alarming, she might indeed have felt herself neglected being left at such a time and having a child here who never went over to see her. To all this he answered

not a word but as soon as he had drank his wine went to Northgate.
[10 days are torn out of the diary at this point. When it resumes Anne is in Market Weighton shortly after her mother's death.]

Saturday 22nd Nov.   Wrote to Mariana (at the house of her father Dr Belcombe in York) wishing her to spend a few days with me at Shibden rather than here, hoping we could contrive to go back together.

Monday 24th Nov.   Mrs George Jackson called and sat an hour with my father, did not see Marian or me. Sat up talking to Marian about Miss Jackson and her brother Mr George Vernon Jackson making remarks on the letters she had received, that it was a mere scheme laid between them to catch her if they could, that Miss Jackson's great friendship was the bridge to go over, that sending her such a packet when they knew my poor mother was still dead in the house was a glaring impropriety which proved their impatient anxiety about their plans, that Miss Jackson saying "He has no fortune it is true but I should <u>rather think</u> that would be no objection with <u>you</u>; he appears to be apprehensive that you think he visits you merely for your <u>Fortune</u>; but let me beg of you in consideration of our friendship to think more favourably both of yourself and of him. As my brother, dear Marian, I feel both for his Honour and his Happiness" etc. etc. unriddled the concern pretty clearly to me, to say nothing of Mr Jackson's letter which I was well persuaded had been written expressly for the purpose to which it was applied. In short after giving Marian much serious advice I told her I could see no good likely to result from any connection with any part of their family and if Miss Jackson never wrote any more Marian will have no real loss to regret. Marian wrote the copy of an answer this morning plainly enough refusing Mr Jackson's attentions, but as affectionate and kind to Miss Jackson as if her friendship formed half the happiness of Marian's life. I advised her giving some assurance that fortune was and ought to be an object of very different import from what Miss Jackson was pleased to surmise.

Tuesday 25th Nov. Mr Inman drank tea with us. I think he is clever in his profession but his general knowledge will never set the Thames on fire. Speaking of Princess Charlotte's death he said it was a business, that she evidently died of exhaustion, that the labour had been too long and she had suffered too much, that Sir Richard Croft (the obstetrician in attendance) knew the consequence of an heir to the throne but if he had another such case tomorrow he would certainly destroy the child to save the mother.

Wednesday 26th Nov. Mr Robinson the attorney called to speak to my father and stayed 10 minutes. Marian and I came upstairs at my father's desire. Sat up talking to Marian about the Jacksons, advised Marian always to consult and tell my father everything.

Thursday 27th Nov. Marian told my father this business about Mr George Jackson and offered to shew him the letters but he would not see them, made no comment but that they wanted the Grange (farm) and he could not spare it yet. Asked Marian if she had told me and hearing that she had, said I was to write the copy of an answer for her. He was pleased however I daresay that Marian had told him.

Friday 28th Nov. Wrote to Miss Marsh (Micklegate, York), said I would accept her offer of a bed, spend a few days with her and be with her about 9 in the evening of next Sunday week (7th December).

Sunday 7th December Got into the coach a little before 6; there was only 1 inside besides myself (in the Birmingham trade, iron goods) a civil, intelligent sort of young man. I asked him his travel expenses: when travelling in his gig he charged his firm a guinea a day, but when travelling by coaches he charged 7s a day and coach-hire, breakfast, tea and supper each 1/6d, dinner 2/- besides wine of which every traveller was expected to take at least a pint at 6/- or 6/6d a bottle, waitress 6d a day, chamber-maid 1s a night and boots 2d. For a gig cleaning 1/6d, 6d or 1/- a night to the ostler, keep of a horse would be about 4/- or rather more.

Took a chaise to Miss Marsh's lodgings, she was at Mr Duffin's and she and Mr Duffin came to give me the meeting. Not expecting to see him his coming increased my agitation, I burst into tears and was obliged to leave the room a little and behaved very foolishly. Miss Marsh (who had read my last letter to Mariana in which I alluded to the misunderstanding between Mr Duffin and me about the letter written to him by Eliza Raine containing a copy of her will) mentioned it to Mr Duffin. I am certainly obliged to her and very glad of it as it has given me uneasiness to *reflect that there should be anything disagreeable towards one whom I am so greatly obliged.*

Monday 8th December Marian came about ½ past 9 to breakfast. She came into my room as soon as I was dressed. Felt a good deal agitated at seeing her yet behaved very well.
A double letter from my aunt Anne (Shibden) enclosing a £10 bank of England note, the remaining ½ of the legacy left me by my uncle Joseph.

Tuesday 9th November Had a few minutes tête-à-tête with Mrs Belcombe (Mariana's mother; we got on the subject of romance; I said I had changed my <u>manners</u> to Mariana as soon as I was properly told of the folly of them, but that my regard for her was still the same as ever (I am not quite so certain of this). Met Eliza and Louisa Belcombe rather formally, 1 and Nantz (Anne Belcombe) and Mrs Belcombe cordially.

Wednesday 10th Nov. Mr Duffin came at 12 to walk with me to Clifton to see Eliza Raine (in Dr Belcombe's mental asylum). She seemed pleased at my visit and expressed a wish for me to go again which I promised. The first thing she said to me was "Well! So you are in mourning for your mother! Is your father going to marry again?" and then inquired after Mr Montagu. She afterwards asked me to take off my hat, felt my face, asked if I ever wore false faces and at last said she "believed it really was my face". She then bade me take off my right-hand glove and observing the thick gold ring Mariana gave me, asked what I had done with the one I used to wear; then looking at my other hand asked significantly after "all my friends". She asked me what I had done with the gold chain she gave me and what with the pocket-handkerchiefs. I told her. When I said I never came to York without calling to see her she answered "What! Never?" and seemed much pleased when I answered "No! Never".

       In our walk there Mr Duffin and I according to our promise to Miss Marsh had all that business over about Eliza's letter to him containing her will which he sent me in February 1816. We mutually explained and he seemed satisfied and appeased. Played whist with Mrs Belcombe and Colonel Milne – I flirted with Harriet then.

Thursday 11th Nov.   Miss Marsh heard from Mrs Bury a quere story about Miss Jane Preston's violently abusing both Mr Charles B. Lawton and Mariana at a party at Lady Vavasour's. J.P. had said Mr CBL was a man of very bad character, that he had broken his first wife's heart and that there had been a connection between him and Mariana during his first wife's lifetime. Nantz took me upstairs to tell me Mariana had had her three stumps of teeth out and was lain down on her mother's bed. I was just going upstairs to see her when Mrs Belcombe preventing me said no-one must disturb her until dinner time. I briefly expressed my opinion that it was not good judgement to prevent my going to her for a minute or two but that I would at any rate comply.

Friday 12th December   Mariana's face bad – worse than yesterday and she had had a bad night in spite of 65 drops of laudanum. However a little before 11 she herself suggested our having a kiss; I thought it dangerous and would willingly have declined the risk but she persisted and by way of excuse to bolt the door sent me downstairs for some paper for that she was going to the close stool. The expedient answered and she tried to laugh me out of my nervousness. I took off my pelisse and got into bed, had a very good kiss, Mariana shewing all due inclination, and in less than seven minutes the door was unbolted and we were alright again.

Just after breakfast Mrs Belcombe said she desired and hoped I would take a bed with them in Petergate; it was agreed I should petition for the little turn-up bed in Mariana and Louisa's room and it was at last so settled.
Saturday 13th Dec.   Found Mariana had just had a very civil note from Mrs Bury (about what Jane Preston had said), heard from Mrs Bury the following conversation:

"Mr Lawton has an idiot brother who sits at the bottom of the table and to whom the property belongs, £6000 a year and indeed we all know how it is spent; only think of Miss Mariana Belcombe who had a good home of her own marrying such a man. Oh! Indeed £6000 a year was not to be lost and not to be got every day; indeed it was well known he only came over for one day to make his offer and there no more till the day before the marriage; there was no time for courtship, and what does it leave the world to suppose but that there must have been either a connection or an engagement between them in the late wife's life time." Dr Belcombe and I had a good deal of conversation about the proper way of managing this affair; he was evidently very warm about it.

Sunday 14th December Just before tea got Miss Maria Duffin to go with me into the front room and play to me on the piano. I said her uncle must be very glad to have her and hoped she would remain with him. She replied "Oh no! He would be very glad to get quit of me." Said she had been a year and a half, a much longer time than she ever intended but that her sisters Miss Delia and Ellen were then on a visit in Hampshire and she only waited to return with them to Ireland. I said something or other about it being better for her to stay where she was and she burst into tears. We then went upstairs to wash our hands.

Slept in the same room with Mariana and Lou in the little turn-up bed by myself, Mariana being afraid of Lou's getting cold as there were not so many bedclothes on it as she had been accustomed to in sleeping in the great bed with Mariana.

Monday 15th Dec. I slept with Mariana and had a very good kiss; pretended to be asleep when Louisa came in. Just before dinner we were all talking over the business (of Jane Preston's insults) and the girls saying they would not be in Jane Preston's place for a good deal, "Oh" said I "I would be in her shoes for 2d and set you all at defiance". They asked me how; I said "Deny the thing flatly, seem abundantly sorry for such a scandal to have been uttered by anyone or imputed to anyone and be abundantly civil". Mariana and Lou personated Mr Duffin and Mrs Darvall and I Jane Preston and we all laughed heartily.

Thursday 16th Dec. [sic] A very good kiss last night before Lou came home from the (assembly) rooms. We were all on tiptoes of expectation when Dr Darvall returned saying he had met Miss Jane P. in the passage, that she was desperately frightened and terribly afraid of her sister *and mother knowing but flatly denied the thing "in toto". Mr Duffin asked us what was to do, giving it as his decided opinion that as she had denied it nothing more could be done. Mr D was evidently much annoyed at my presuming to dissent, more particularly as Mariana seemed to agree with me and so did Nantz and Eli. Luckily Milne came in and was so entirely on my side of the argument that Mr Duffin seemed more reconciled (to requesting an apology). This Lady Vavasour (who has brought all the estate and on whose account her husband Mr North, a moneyless officer, changed his name and became Sir Henry Vavasour of Melbourne in this county) begins her note with a little I and spells the words generally and principally with only 1 l e.g. generaly, principaly.*

Friday 17th December A good kiss just before getting up. Letter of condolence on the death of my poor mother from Helen Waterton (from her brother's Charles Waterton's, Walton Hall near Wakefield). Lou and I sat perhaps a couple of hours together and she gave me my 2nd lesson in Parkhurst's Hebrew Grammar. The language seems very easy and I think I could soon get a tolerable knowledge of it. She can read a chapter in Genesis by herself with the assistance of a lexicon.

* I called on Mrs Frances Swann just to say goodbye and stayed ½ hour at the Duffins' and took leave of Mrs Duffin. Miss Marsh had called while we were out and Mrs Belcombe told her she was not at all satisfied with what had been done about Jane Preston who had got off much too easily. Anne, Eli, Lou and Col. And Mrs Milne drank tea at the John Rapers'; Mariana and I had delivered the*

invitation. We sat up talking so long that Lou came before we got into bed.

Thursday 18th Dec.   A kiss this morning just before getting up. Took leave of Miss Maria Duffin whom I think a very nice girl – she is perhaps about 5 feet 7 inches, has a very fine figure and is near 30.

Walked with Mr Duffin to Clifton to see poor Eliza Raine. She behaved (as she had done before) more idiotically than madly. At my request we were left a little by ourselves. At first she said she should take no insolence, no impertinence from me, that I had never done her any good and if I was impertinent we should come to blows. After a somewhat stern remonstrance on my part she said I had always thought nothing of her, that I might have genius, I might have talent but that I had made a bad use of them and indeed the world thought me a fool.

She then grew more kind and asked to feel my face, to pinch my nose and feel my eyes. She said she believed it really was my face, seemed pleased to see me and desired me to sit by her on the sopha. At this moment Mr Duffin and Mrs Clarkson the housekeeper returned and I took my leave. Eliza had tears in her eyes – the only sensitive symptom I have observed since her malady.

Went with Miss Marsh to call on Fisher (the Norcliffe's estate manager) who had just had a letter from the Norcliffes dated Bruxelles. Charlotte had been very ill at Nice but was out of danger, Isabella was pretty well again but Emily still very much indisposed from a bad cold caught by going on the barouche box on the journey from Berne to Bruxelles.

Got home only just in time to dress for dinner. As soon as we left the dining room went upstairs into our own room and sat talking very cozily to Lou about Mariana, Lawton, Charles and one thing or another. She as well as Anne strongly suspects that neither Mariana nor I would much regret the loss of Charles but that we look forward to the thing and in the event of it certainly mean to live together. Lou and I have joked about it several times, I asking if she thought I might hope to come into possession of Mariana in ten years, a decade! Both Lou and Nantz think I may say 5 years instead of 10 and ½ a decade is become quite a joke among us. I have before told Lou I thought I had better take her on a running lease till Mariana was ready for me. Lou agrees and we are very good friends. What Anne thinks of it all I cannot say; she certainly is as fond of me as ever and would gladly do as much for me now as she did at Shibden last November.

  On going down into the drawing room and speaking to Mariana found her very low and in tears – she wondered how I could leave her so long the last night and said she should be jealous of Lou. Though I laughed at the thing at first I soon perceived it more real than I imagined. A little after 11 we all retired. Lou being away we had a glorious opportunity for a kiss, but the annoyance occasioned by my attention to Lou had made Mariana cool, unwell and out of sorts and I let her be as quiet as possible.

Friday 19th December No kiss this morning as Mariana did not feel well last night tho' Lou did not get home from the Serjeantson's till 1 o'clock. Busy packing all the morning, Mariana sat by me. Talked over my adventures *in former days; Mariana said had she known them she would never have been introduced to me. Mariana wanted a kiss but I said it was too dangerous, that I really had not courage and that we had better practise a little self-denial.*

Took my seat in the True Blue coach and drove off for Leeds as the clock struck 2. We reached Leeds and stopped at the Golden Lion at ½ past 6. After at least ¼ mile's wet walk through dirty, busy streets they told me I could not secure a place in the mail till 4 in the morning and that they were so full they had not a bed to spare me. Sent for my friend the chamber-maid [who] put me into a parlour that would not be wanted till 10 and let me have a snug little bedroom at the extremity of the house on the 3rd floor.

Sunday 21st December Wrote to Mariana to announce my safe arrival and to say I had ordered four horses at the Rose and Crown (Briggate, Leeds) to be ready for her at one next Friday. My uncle and aunt let me into my aunt Lister's great grief for the loss of her husband. It appears she is not satisfied with my uncle's having left her the house and premises as they stand for her life and an annuity of three hundred pounds in lieu of her thirds and the thousand pounds he has had of hers. She told my uncle only a fortnight after the funeral "Good came out of evil and it was well that the £3000 left her in her father's will was fixed as it was otherwise my uncle Joseph would have taken that also." Last Tuesday she told my uncle she had asked Mr Wiglesworth (the solicitor) and he said she could claim her thirds as there was no bar. My uncle calmly replied that she knew that was not her husband's intent, she had seen the will before his death and then said she was satisfied.

This she acknowledged but said Joseph was ill and she did not like to say anything. Here the matter ended.

Tuesday 23rd December   Did nothing in the afternoon but count my money to see what I had spent while away. My aunt gave me an account of what she had paid for my mourning which amounted to £8-0-6d, the 6d being abated. I paid her £8, she having first given me £5 and my uncle having also given me £5. Talked over family affairs, about my father, etc.

Thursday 25th Dec.   We all went to morning church and stayed the sacrament; assisted my aunt in reading prayers in the afternoon; in the evening read aloud sermons 8, 9 Hoole.

Friday 26th December Mariana arrived here at 5 by the kitchen clock, ¾ past 4 by Halifax and ¼ past 4 by Leeds and York. She brought me a tassie seal, a new moon rising over the sea, motto "je ne change qu'en appearance" Mariana told us after tea what a narrow escape Mr Charles Lawton had had the other day of being shot. In getting over a hedge something caught the trigger, the gun went off and the contents only just missed. A similar accident I understand occurred to him just before Mariana and Louisa left Lawton and his glove and waistcoat were a good deal burnt.

Saturday 27th Dec.   A very good kiss last night though Mariana's cousin came last Sunday and was not quite well. An account of the death of poor Emily Norcliffe in a letter from Isabella Norcliffe: "my father is in such a state of agitation and grief that he cannot leave his bed and I dread the shock will be more than he can support." Speaking of poor Charlotte: "For some time she has had a spitting of matter – it was the same as that which poor Charles (Best) had been accustomed to expectorate. A Scotch physician arrived and what he has given her has done her good though we are still in a state of great alarm about her." This melancholy letter, this unexpected shock so afflicted and unsettled me I could do nothing all the day. This is indeed a bitter day. Poor Emily!

Sunday 28th December Mariana had a very good kiss last night; mine was not quite so good but I had a very nice one this morning.

Just as the dinner things were going out John Morgan the coachman arrived with a letter from Mr Charles Lawton saying he was happy to find Mariana so unexpectedly on her journey, that he had set off from Lawton the moment he received her letter, anf that she might not be detained on the road he had sent John forward by the coach to tell her to take 4 posters (horses), set off immediately and travel as fast as she could to meet him in good time in Manchester this evening, adding that if she had been in any other direction he believed he should have met her there himself though the distance had been twice as far.

It was after two before John got here; he had his dinner to get and to go back again to the White Lion to order the carriage, we not having had room for it here. The poor fellow however, his frost-bitten face all colours, sent in a message to say his mistress must go. It was bitter cold, the roads dreadfully slippery, Blackstone Edge to cross and no moon – but his mistress understood the necessity. All was got ready and they were off from our door a few minutes before 4.

Monday 29th Dec.   the postman this morning brought the news of the death of Mr John Greenwood of Cross Hills who was thrown from his horse. Mr J.G. was the younger son to the late William Greenwood Esquire, banker of Leeds, aged 24.

Wednesday 31st Dec.   Was all the morning writing the copy of a letter of condolence to Mrs Norcliffe on the death of poor Emily.

End

www.ingramcontent.com/pod-product-compliance
Lightning Source LLC
Chambersburg PA
CBHW071501160426
43195CB00013B/2176